# Understanding
# PEOPLE IN THE PAST

*A Teacher's Guide to*
*Historic Scotland Properties*

HISTORIC SCOTLAND

FIRST PUBLISHED 1995
© copyright Historic Scotland

ACKNOWLEDGMENTS
This book is based on a text by Sydney Wood,
Northern College of Education, Aberdeen, and
edited by Marion Fry, Education Officer,
Historic Scotland, Longmore House, Salisbury
Place, Edinburgh EH9 1SH.
Additional contributions from Historic Scotland
staff and Gordon Jarvie Editorial.
Design and layout by Jim Hutcheson.

ISBN 0 7480 1226 5

## Foreword by

LORD JAMES DOUGLAS-HAMILTON MP, *Minister for Education at the Scottish Office.*

Historic Scotland has some of the best castles, abbeys, prehistoric and industrial monuments in the country. I know them well – and remember how in my youth they fired me with enthusiasm for our history.

So, as Minister for Education in Scotland, I welcome Historic Scotland's initiative in producing this attractive book. It introduces teachers, and others who are interested, to the potential of sites in Historic Scotland's care. It selects six properties in different parts of Scotland to show in more detail what teachers can do to bring to life Scotland's rich heritage of historic buildings and monuments. The selected sites represent different types of building and cover a period ranging from early settlers in Scotland to the 19th century. The case studies illustrate different approaches, applicable to ancient monuments and historic buildings whether or not they are in the care of Historic Scotland.

Scottish schoolchildren have always had good opportunities to study the environment outwith their classrooms. The investigations which pupils do for Standard Grade have shown the usefulness of active exploration. The 5–14 development programme is emphasising the value of giving pupils direct experience of the Scottish landscape, its fine buildings and many collections housed in museums, galleries and historic houses. I hope that this book helps teachers to tap that potential – not only for the obvious historical parts of the environmental studies curriculum but also for art, religious education, mathematics and other aspects of the 5–14 guidelines.

*James Douglas-Hamilton*

HISTORIC SCOTLAND
*Spring 1995*

# Historic Scotland's Services for Schools

Historic Scotland is a government agency which works on behalf of the Secretary of State for Scotland. Its task is to protect Scotland's built heritage for future generations and to present it to the public. Throughout Scotland, there are over 330 properties in Historic Scotland's care including prehistoric sites, castles, abbeys, industrial buildings and a lighthouse. Historic Scotland is also responsible for scheduling monuments, listing buildings of special architectural or historical importance, conservation work, research into conservation techniques and archaeological projects.

## Free Educational Visits Scheme

Historic Scotland offers free entry for school parties to its properties where there is normally a charge, with the exceptions of Edinburgh Castle in June, July and August and Stirling Castle in July and August. Application forms should be sent directly to the custodian of the site at least 10 days before the visit. Children must be supervised throughout the visit with at least one adult for every 12 children.

## Educational Resources

School Packs containing background information, visual material and on-site activities are available for Caerlaverock Castle, Craignethan Castle, Doune Castle, Dunfermline Abbey, Edzell Castle, Elgin Cathedral, Fort George, Jedburgh Abbey, Linlithgow Palace and Stirling Castle. Further booklets and School Packs offering ideas and information for teachers relating to specific sites are currently being developed.

## Further Information

An up-to-date list of publications, application forms and information leaflets on school visits is available from The Education Officer, Historic Scotland, Longmore House, Salisbury Place, Edinburgh EH9 1SH. Tel: 0131-668 8732

DIRLETON CASTLE - CHILDREN ON SITE

# Contents

# Links to the 5-14 Guidelines

## Environmental Studies and other curricular areas

The attainment outcome 'Understanding People in the Past' forms a natural focus for fieldwork and follow-up activities but a visit to a historic site is also relevant to many features of the Environmental Studies guidelines and other curricular areas. This section outlines some ideas, many of which are developed in later sections of the book through activities pursued both on and after fieldwork, and shows how a visit to a historic site can be the focus of a very full range of curricular activities.

### Understanding People in the Past

STUDYING PEOPLE, EVENTS AND SOCIETIES OF SIGNIFICANCE IN THE PAST

Many of the sites have links with important events and personalities in the history of Scotland. Pupils are expected to give serious attention to the Scottish context which is of great significance in helping them make sense of their environment.

UNDERSTANDING CHANGE AND CONTINUITY, CAUSE AND EFFECT

Many sites were exploited at different times in different ways and at one site pupils can see evidence from a wide range of time. Visiting a historic site encourages pupils to ask 'when' and 'why' questions that often lead to a discussion of causes and results.

UNDERSTANDING TIME AND HISTORICAL SEQUENCE

Through a careful study, including relating site work to contextual knowledge, pupils should be able to place sites in time in relation to one another and/or to other items of evidence.

UNDERSTANDING THE NATURE OF HISTORICAL EVIDENCE

Pupils will be studying the actual materials shaped by people of the past. A visit to a site will enable them to come to their own conclusions regarding the interpretation of the evidence before them and in some cases lead them to understand that answers are not always easy to find on the basis of the evidence available.

CONSIDERING THE MEANING OF HERITAGE

The work of Historic Scotland in protecting sites for future generations and making them accessible to the public is brought to the pupils' attention and they can come to their own conclusions about the value of this work.

### Understanding People and Place

ASPECTS OF THE PHYSICAL AND BUILT ENVIRONMENT

Pupils will examine and record aspects of the site in relation to its surrounding environment.

WAYS IN WHICH PLACES HAVE AFFECTED PEOPLE AND PEOPLE HAVE USED AND AFFECTED PLACES

This aspect would be central to a visit.

LOCATIONS, LINKAGES AND NETWORKS

Pupils may consider reasons for the monuments being placed where they are.

MAKING AND USING MAPS

The creation or completion of outline maps and plans will form an essential part of work at many sites.

### Understanding and Using Technology in Society

The different features of the Technology attainment outcome - technology and human needs, technology and demand for resources, technology as it affects lifestyle, technology to control the environment, and technology responding to values and scientific progress - may often be implemented through a historical study. On some sites, for example where there is a watermill, the technology is clearly visible and its needs can be seen shaping the environment, affecting life styles, needing resources and eventually being overtaken by scientific progress.

UNDERSTANDING AND USING THE DESIGN PROCESS

Activities and experiments such as designing an effective missile-firing machine or assessing which type of waterwheel is most effective may stem from a visit and would form part of the follow-up work. A site visit also often offers an opportunity for designing souvenirs associated with the monument.

### Understanding Living Things and the Processes of Life

THE INTERACTION OF LIVING THINGS WITH THEIR ENVIRONMENT

Pupils can investigate which animals, birds, insects and plants are attracted to old buildings. Some sites have interesting period gardens while others are located near ancient woods or riverside trails.

### Understanding Energy and Forces

PROPERTIES AND USES OF ENERGY

Lifestyles of people in the past provide a context for exploring issues of lighting and heating which can lead to experiments on return to the classroom.

FORCES AND THEIR EFFECTS

The moving of huge standing stones and the raising of them to an upright position, or the work involved in building impressive towers and cathedrals offers an excellent focus for pupil investigation on return to the classroom.

## Other Curricular Areas

### EXPRESSIVE ARTS

Dramatic re-enactments, role-play, dance, music-making, sketching and detailed drawing may be developed either during a visit to a historic site, or on return to the classroom.

### ENGLISH LANGUAGE

Language will be used in a variety of ways with opportunities for discussion, creative and functional writing and roleplay.

### RELIGIOUS AND MORAL EDUCATION

Many sites have been regarded as sacred places over a long period of time. A visit to such sites encourages consideration of the place of religion in different societies. At cathedrals and abbeys, pupils will be able to look for symbols and artefacts associated with the Christian faith which have been passed down over hundreds of years.

## Historic Sites and the 5-14 Attainment Targets

The attainment targets describe a sequence of work. The preparation for the visit itself and the follow-up to it, form an ideal focus for such a flow of activities. The visit can be prepared and structured with these targets in mind and with the levels described in them shaping the differentiation of pupil work.

### PLANNING

Prior to visits, pupils consider what they would like to find out, developing key questions to pursue. They consider how they might be able to find out what they will need for this.

### COLLECTING EVIDENCE

This can be done on site and using follow-up resources.

### RECORDING AND PRESENTING

Both on site and subsequent to the visit a variety of recording and presenting skills may be developed.

### INTERPRETING AND EVALUATING

On site discussion and follow-up work inevitably involve making sense of what has been studied.

### KNOWLEDGE AND UNDERSTANDING

As well as relating to the key features of Understanding People in the Past, features of People and Place, Science, Technology, and Religious and Moral Education may also be relevant.

### DEVELOPING INFORMED ATTITUDES

Work in the environment outside school is ideal for this purpose. Issues of conservation and heritage will flow naturally from fieldwork.

**STIRLING CASTLE**, ONE OF THE MOST POPULAR SITES FOR SCHOOL VISITS. A NEW INTRODUCTORY DISPLAY ON THE HISTORY OF THE CASTLE WAS OPENED DURING 1994.

# Topics, sites, and the 5-14 timeline

Although many sites span several periods, the following table highlights sites which would be appropriate to visit if pupils are studying an aspect of the period listed. Posters, slides and information packs for major sites may be available for use in class if visiting is not possible.

| BC - 400 AD | 400 - 1450 | 1450 - 1700 |
| --- | --- | --- |

## The Ancient World to 5th Century AD

**Early settlers** - Skara Brae (Orkney), Knap of Howar (Orkney)

**Bronze Age** - Machrie Moor Stone Circle ( Arran), a number of monuments in the Kilmartin valley (Argyll), Clava Cairns (near Inverness), Cairnpapple Hill (Lothian), Jarlshof (Shetland)

**Iron Age** - Cairnpapple (Lothian), Jarlshof (Shetland), Mousa Broch (Shetland), souterrains and earthhouses such as at Ardestie and Carlungie in Tayside and Culsh in Grampian

**Romans** - Antonine Wall - especially Bearsden Bathhouse and Rough Castle fort

SKARA BRAE

MACHRIE MOOR STONE CIRCLE

MOUSA BROCH

## The Middle Ages (400 - 1450)

**Picts** - Meigle Museum, St Vigeans Sculptured Stones (near Arbroath), Aberlemno churchyard, Elgin Cathedral, Sueno's Stone (Forres)

**Vikings** - Jarlshof (Shetland), Brough of Birsay (Orkney), Rothesay Castle

**Wars with England** - Stirling Castle, Bothwell Castle, Caerlaverock Castle (near Dumfries), Kildrummy Castle, Linlithgow Palace, Jedburgh Abbey, Dunfermline Abbey

SUENO'S STONE

## Renaissance, Reformation and the Age of Discovery (1450 - 1700)

**The times of James IV** - Linlithgow Palace, Stirling Castle, Edinburgh Castle

**The times of Mary Queen of Scots** - Linlithgow Palace, Stirling Castle, Dundrennan Abbey, Loch Leven Castle, Edinburgh Castle, Balvenie Castle, Hermitage Castle, Dundrennan Abbey

**Renaissance** - Stirling Castle, Caerlaverock Castle, Edzell Castle, Huntingtower Castle (near Perth)

**Reformation** - St Andrews Castle and Cathedral, abbeys

ST ANDREWS CASTLE (VISITOR CENTRE)

| **1700 - 1900** | **1900 - 2000** |
|---|---|

### The Age of Revolutions (1700 - 1900)

**Industry** - Click Mill at Dounby (Orkney), Bonawe Ironworks (Taynuilt), Dallas Dhu Distillery (Forres), New Abbey Cornmill (near Dumfries)

**The 1745 Uprising** - Corgarff Castle, Ruthven Barracks, Fort George

**The Clearances** - Blackhouse at Arnol (Lewis)

RUTHVEN BARRACKS

BLACKHOUSE AT ARNOL (INTERIOR)

### Twentieth Century

**World Wars 1 and 2** - Independent war museums at Edinburgh Castle, Fort George, Stirling Castle

**Uses of historic monuments today** - all sites

### The local area - Other sites to visit

As well as Historic Scotland sites which are located throughout the country there are also numerous sites in the care of the National Trust for Scotland and in independent ownership. The local REEF (Regional Environmental Education Forum) directory, which is updated regularly, is a useful guide to sites in the local area. The *Exploring Scotland's Heritage* series published by HMSO gives details of sites on a regional basis based on the records of the Royal Commission on Ancient and Historical Monuments of Scotland. *Exploring Scotland's Historic Sites* by Dr Elsie Farquharson, published by the Social Studies Department of Northern College (1994), is also a very useful source for identifying local monuments and sites of special interest. A directory of all sites in the care of Historic Scotland is also available.

# Making the Most of a Visit

**FORT GEORGE –** THE MASSIVE DEFENCES OF FORT GEORGE, FOR EXAMPLE, MAKE LITTLE SENSE IF THEY ARE NOT SEEN AS THE HIGHLY EXPENSIVE RESPONSE OF A VERY ALARMED GOVERNMENT TO THE EVENTS OF 1745-6.

**TOWER AT INCHCOLM –** THE PRE-VISIT WILL HELP THE TEACHER DECIDE IF THERE ARE ANY PARTS OF THE MONUMENT WHICH SHOULD BE OUT OF BOUNDS.

**MELROSE ABBEY –** PUPILS SHOULD BE ABLE TO RECOGNISE THE NAMES FOR THE MAIN FEATURES IN AN ABBEY BEFORE VISITING THE SITE.

## Preparation

Fieldwork on site should form an integral part of a study, building on what has gone before and feeding into what follows. It generally makes most sense to visit a site when pupils are able to bring to it a considerable amount of contextual knowledge and understanding. It may also be necessary to develop and practise skills such as interpreting plans or ways of recording measurements prior to the visit and a grasp of specialist vocabulary may also be required.

Pupils should be reminded of safety issues and the potential dangers of a historic site.

### Preliminary visit to the site

Teachers are encouraged to visit the site prior to the visit with pupils. The custodian will be pleased to discuss practical matters such as parking, toilets, safety issues and timing. A preliminary visit, which is free of charge, also gives the teacher the opportunity to assess any support materials which are available to decide how these should be adapted to suit the needs of the pupils.

## On-site

Where possible, pupils on site should be engaged in purposeful activities that are clearly understood and supported by necessary resources. Whether activities are framed in detail or left as broad problems/issues to investigate will depend on the site, on the ability of the pupils and on the purpose of going there. There is much to be said for pupils working in small groups of two or three, giving mutual support and benefiting from discussion and sharing tasks. Some pupils may benefit more from being faced with a problem which they have to subdivide into facets that require research rather than completing a worksheet which presents them with a complete sequence of detailed tasks.

The time spent on site will vary according to the nature of the site, the age of the pupils and even the weather. A site as rich as Stirling Castle could justify spending much of a day, although there is always the danger of confusing pupils by a determination to look at everything rather than focusing on an issue directly relevant to a project. If a site is local, or there is not a lot of cost involved in visiting, then several shorter visits could be made to enable pupils to focus on developing different skills and exploring various aspects of the site.

School Packs, Site Profiles and Quizzes are available for a number of sites. If these are not available, the following questions may provide a starting point for the study of most sites.

Why was this building sited here?
How long has there been a building on this site?
What evidence is there for changes which have taken place on this site?
What does this building tell us about the people who lived here / in this area?
How is this building used today?
Do visitors damage this site?
Should this building be protected for the future?

ABOVE: THERE ARE AROUND 1,000,000
VISITORS TO EDINBURGH CASTLE EACH YEAR.

## Follow-up work

A well planned visit produces ideas and understanding which may be exploited in a number of ways :

**Reporting** - If pupils have been pursuing different tasks, this is clearly needed but even if the same tasks have been followed, it is worthwhile to check on full understanding and careful observation.

**Discussing** - Through discussion of what has been seen, confusions can be sorted out and the whys and wherefores can be considered.

**Recording** - Information gathered needs to be recorded clearly and systematically.

**Presenting** - An attractive wall display in map or pictorial form, a re-enactment of a past event, the production of a trail or guided tour for younger pupils are a few possibilities here.

**Researching** - The visit may well raise issues about people, places, events and technology which will lead to further exploration.

**Experimenting** - Opportunities will arise depending on the type of site and issues raised.

LIVING HISTORY EVENT AT DOUNE CASTLE

# Checklist

*Teachers may like to use the following checklist when planning a visit.*

6 WEEKS BEFORE THE VISIT

☐ Choose a provisional date.    Check availability on the school calendar.

☐ Check that the site will be open.    Telephone the custodian.

☐ Obtain approval for the outing.    Consult your Head Teacher/AHT.

☐ Arrange transport.    Provisionally book a coach or the school minibus. Organise a driver for the latter.

☐ Book a free visit.    Photocopy Historic Scotland application form inside the back cover of this book and send it directly to the site you wish to visit. Phone 0131- 668 8831 for details if you do not know the address.

☐ Arrange helpers.    Organise accompanying staff or parents (1 adult to 12 pupils)

4 WEEKS BEFORE THE VISIT

☐ Inform pupils of visit.    Discuss visit with pupils and inform them of date.

☐ Obtain parental consent.    Follow school or regional policy guidelines. Mention any cost involved, clothing and footwear required, and whether pupils should bring a packed lunch. Give a week's deadline for return of completed forms.

☐ Arrange cover    For classes you will miss or for pupils excluded from visit.

☐ Other in-school arrangements.    In secondary schools: circulate a list of participating pupils to other departments. Inform the school meals service of reduced numbers and arrange a supply of packed lunches for pupils in receipt of free school meals.

SHORTLY BEFORE THE VISIT

☐ Prepare pupils for visit.    Explain purpose of visit. Select and photocopy activity sheets required. Give older pupils the opportunity to choose the topic they wish to investigate on site and to plan their approach.

☐ Assemble equipment.    Clipboards, spare pencils, measuring tapes, camera, basic first-aid kit, information sheets for staff and helpers.

**Teachers are strongly encouraged to visit the property before they take pupils. This will provide an opportunity for locating toilets, familiarising themselves with the site and identifying any potential dangers. The custodian will be happy to answer any questions about the history of the site and site-based teaching materials which are available may be viewed.**

# Prehistoric Sites

## *Opportunities offered*

The 5-14 Environmental Studies Guidelines define 'Ancient Times' as going up to the beginning of the 5th century AD. A number of sites in the care of Historic Scotland fit into this category, including early houses such as those found at Knap of Howar and Skara Brae, burial mounds, standing stones, hill forts, souterrains, brochs, and Roman remains such as the bathhouse at Bearsden and Rough Castle fort on the Antonine Wall.

Many prehistoric sites reflect different periods having buildings added and adapted over hundreds and even thousands of years. Jarlshof in Shetland, for example, not only has evidence pointing to about 2400 BC, when the site was inhabited by neolithic farmers, but also has evidence from the Bronze Age, the Iron Age, Viking times and beyond. Likewise Cairnpapple Hill in West Lothian has evidence of ceremonies and burials taking place there over more than two thousand years between about 2800 BC and 500 BC.

The settlers of Mesolithic times (from about 9000 BC to about 4000 BC), who lived by hunting, fishing and eating wild fruits, have left us little but a few stone tools that they used, as well as midden remains. The early farmers, who learned to grow and harvest crops and domesticate animals, tended to stay longer in one place than their predecessors. They, and their successors who developed the ability to make tools from copper, bronze and eventually iron, have left us much more evidence. Remains of their houses and burial monuments can be found throughout Scotland.

A truly remarkable range of stone circles and standing stones remains on the Scottish landscape. It is very difficult to date the stone circles precisely, yet it is very likely that the first stone circles were the creation of our Neolithic ancestors and date from about 3000 BC. All represent a considerable amount of physical effort by the well-organised groups of people who created them. The stones often came from a distance, having been dragged by many people before being levered into a secure position. The labour involved was undertaken by people who had not mastered the making of metal tools but made skilled use of implements of stone, wood and bone. The sheer scale of some of the structures indicates how important they must have been to the early farmers who created them.

The case study in this section focuses on the Standing Stones at Callanish. It is hoped that teachers will be able to adapt the approach and ideas described here to other prehistoric sites.

## Recommended reading

Historic Scotland Guidebooks and information leaflets for individual sites. The colour guidebooks to Skara Brae and Jarlshof are especially recommended.

### *For teachers*

A Ritchie : *Scotland BC*, HMSO 1988
C R Wickham-Jones : *Scotland's First Settlers*, Batsford 1994
*Environmental Studies 5 - 14 : Staff Development Support Pack*, SCCC 1994

### *For pupils*

FICTION
B Ball : *Stone Age Magic*, Penguin 1989
A class on a museum visit bring two stone-age children into the present.
K Fidler : *The Boy with the Bronze Axe*, Puffin 1972
Life at Skara Brae.
R Sutcliff : *Shifting Sands*, H Hamilton 1977
Life at Skara Brae.
R Sutcliff : *Eagle of the Ninth*, H Hamilton 1954
A young Roman centurion's life on Britain's northern frontier.
NON-FICTION
F Jarvie : *The Romans in Scotland*, HMSO Scotties 1994
An information book for 8 - 12-year-olds, with activities.
*Lifting by Levers*, Wayland 1993
One of a series of books looking at how things work. Reading Age 9-11.

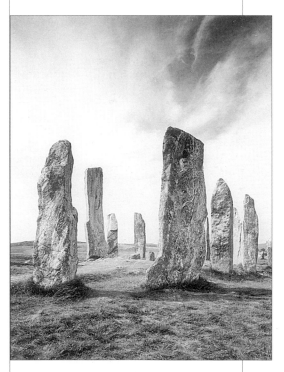

SOME INTERESTING SITES MAY BE ON PRIVATE LAND, AS IS THE CASE WITH SOME OF THE OTHER STONE CIRCLES IN THE NEIGHBOURHOOD OF THE STANDING STONES AT CALLANISH. VISITORS MUST KEEP TO MARKED PATHS AND IN ALL CASES THE PERMISSION OF LANDOWNERS MUST BE SOUGHT BEFORE THESE SITES ARE VISITED.

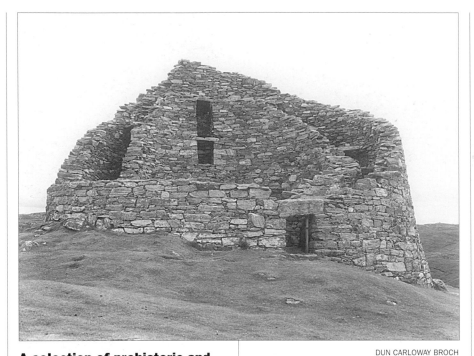

DUN CARLOWAY BROCH

CLAVA CAIRNS

CASTLELAW FORT

CAIRNPAPPLE HILL

## A selection of prehistoric and Roman sites in the care of Historic Scotland

**Skara Brae**, Orkney. The first inhabitants were living in this village around 3100 BC.

**Jarlshof**, Shetland. Remains of Bronze Age village of oval stone huts. Also Iron Age broch and wheelhouses.

**Cairnpapple Hill**, West Lothian. Ceremonial and burial site dating from between 2800 BC and 500 BC.

**Clava Cairns**, near Inverness. Two chambered cairns and a ring cairn in a row, each surrounded by a circle of stones. Of late neolithic or Early Bronze Age times.

**Dun Carloway Broch**, Lewis. One of the best examples of a broch tower in Scotland.

**Castlelaw Fort** and Souterrain, Lothian. An Iron Age hill fort with a souterrain built in one of the ditches.

**Bearsden Roman Bath House**, Strathclyde. Built in the 2nd century AD to serve a small fort on the Antonine Wall.

SKARA BRAE

BEARSDEN ROMAN BATH HOUSE

JARLSHOF

CALLANISH

## Callanish Standing Stones

Of all the groups of standing stones that it is still possible to visit in Britain, the great stones at Callanish on the Isle of Lewis form one of the most impressive. Believed to be older than Stonehenge, the ring was constructed around 5000 years ago. At the very centre of the ring stands a huge stone over four metres high. A great stone avenue was added to its north side and single lines of stone point east, south and west. In the eastern half of the ring lies a stone-lined burial chamber of a later period which is reached from a passageway entered between two of the uprights. The stones at Callanish are very visible from the sealoch nearby and some claim that the site was placed here because it was a good place to see the moon skimming over the hills to the south. Callanish is not an isolated stone circle; remains of other stone circles can be found nearby.

Callanish has been a special place for thousands of years. Excavation of the site has shown that it was used by people even before the first stones were put in place. Underneath the stones, archaeologists have found remains of ancient fields used to grow wheat or barley. Ridges had been made to increase the depth of the soil and to improve drainage.

Many people must have lived in the area. Early settlers on island and coastal sites could exploit both the land and the sea for food. We must be careful, however, not to jump to the conclusion that early people preferred islands. Sites of historic interest survive better on land which is suitable for rough grazing rather than on good farming land where there have been agricultural improvements. At Callanish, for example, you can see 'lazy beds' (the means used in the Western Isles to make an area of land more suitable for growing) exactly where stones are missing in the avenue of standing stones.

There is evidence for many changes in the landscape around Callanish since it was first in use as a ceremonial site. The sea has risen, the coast has been eroded and peat, which started to appear about 900 BC, eventually covered all the stones less than 5 feet high. You can still see the remains of homes which were built in this area in the late 18th and early 19th century. The inhabitants of these houses were moved into the present settlement just to the north in the mid 19th century at the same time as the site was cleared of peat. It is estimated that nowadays about 20,000 people visit the stones each year. A visitor centre, opening Summer 1995, is being built on a site near the stones but not within sight of them.

The purpose of Callanish remains a mystery and it, like many other prehistoric sites, provides a fascinating opportunity for children to use their imaginations as they consider the many possibilities. Pupils should be able to provide their own suggestions based on the evidence of the site and information boards which are located nearby. They will not be expected to understand all the difficulties of interpreting such a site but they should be able to formulate their own ideas based on the evidence that they find.

## Making the most of a visit

PREPARATION

Pupils' investigation of this prehistoric site will be enriched if they have an understanding of the great revolution that occurred in Neolithic times. The development of farming made a great difference in the lives of early people and had a powerful impact on the landscape. An understanding of the kinds of stone tools and weapons available to Neolithic people and of their way of life would also be very helpful.

Before the visit, the location of the site could be considered at a level appropriate to the pupils' understanding. Pupils could note its distance from the school, how the site is shown on different types of maps, as well as considering different ways of going there. Before the visit, pupils could collect different kinds of stones which could be examined and tested in order to establish their feel, colour, relative weights, degree of hardness and rates at which they absorb water. The stones could also be tested to see how good they would have been at pounding grain, and scraping or breaking up ground. The results of findings could be recorded.

Some prehistoric sites are very sensitive and great care should be taken not to damage them. At Callanish, for example, visitors are encouraged to walk round the perimeter of the site and not to enter the centre. If pupils are closely supervised they may go closer to the stones but it would be good for teachers to consider with all pupils the effect that visitors have on the site and to remind them of how unique the site is and why it is protected.

ON-SITE INVESTIGATIONS

### Why were the stones placed here?

Why was this site chosen for the standing stones?
Why would this area have been a good place for Neolithic people to live?
Why do you think so many good sites dating from early times are found on islands?
What do you think this site was used for?
Look for evidence to show how this site has changed since the stones were first put in place here.

### What remains of the site today?

The age and ability of pupils will determine how far the problem of devising and recording a plan of the site can be left to pupils to solve or whether it needs to consist of a sequence of smaller tasks to be followed. The more the pupils can discuss and resolve the problem, the better. At its simplest, however, the task can consist of a provided plan to be completed, coloured and labelled. Geographical and mathematical skills will be developed here.

Pupils should consider
 • How many stones are there?
 • Are they spaced out equally?
 • Where is the biggest stone?
 • How might Neolithic people have created a circle shape? (Here a central stick and the use of string can be provided to help the working out of a solution.)
 • How are the lines of stones radiating out laid out in terms of the points of a compass?
 • How would you draw a scale drawing of the site? (Consider how different scales of measurement serve different purposes.)

### What sort of stones have been used?

The study of the stones provides opportunities for geological, scientific and technological, mathematical, language and expressive arts skills to be developed.

Pupils could
 • Take photographs of individual and groups of stones
 • Estimate the height of stones
 • Sketch stones, paying attention to their texture
 • Compare the stones with small ones previously studied
 • Explore the area to see if there are stones nearby that are similar/ different.
 • Discuss/note down ideas about how the stones were moved to the site and levered into position
 • List/choose adjectives that suitably describe the stones

### What sort of burial site is there?

What sort of person or people would have been buried on such a site?
How has the burial place been constructed?
What shape and size is it?
(This will involve designing and labelling a plan or labelling one which has been provided.)

### Are there other forms of life on this site?

What plants are growing on the stones?
Do different plants grow in different parts of the site?
What words describe these plants best?
What animals and insects can you find in the area around the stones?
What difference would it make to plants and animals if the stones were cleaned regularly?

### How has this site changed over time?

A site like Callanish has been used by people over a long period of time in different ways. Visiting a site which has such a long history stimulates reflection about the lives of people in the past and encourages young people to consider what value the site has for them and for people in the future. Pupils could also consider the impact that visitors have on the site.

On site pupils could
 • discuss why the stones were placed there
 • suggest why the stones radiating from the circle were added at a later date
 • search for evidence to show how the site has been changed because of the number of visitors
 • discuss whether visitors should be kept at a distance from the site
 • look for evidence to show how the stones themselves have changed over time
 • suggest what could be done to protect the stones and the site from erosion.
 • listen to or tell a story on the site. Short extracts from historical fiction could be read out, stories about magic or the seasons might be told, words helpful in establishing the atmosphere of the place could be

noted down, and the hopes and fears of the people of the past could be discussed.

FOLLOWING UP FIELDWORK

Fieldwork is a data-gathering exercise. On return to the classroom the data needs to be reviewed, discussed and recorded. Further data may need to be added from other sources. Possibilities for follow-up work include

**Understanding People in the Past**
• Further research into other aspects of Neolithic life or a study of other similar sites perhaps in a European or even worldwide context.

• Creating a clear record of the site in the way an archaeologist might record some of the details(see right).

• Developing a timeline using numbers, words and pictures to place the site in relation to other key features of the past.

**English Language**
• Imaginative writing in story or poem form using words and ideas built upon the visit.

**Expressive Arts**
• Expressing ideas, feelings and thoughts by drawing, painting, modelling, collage work.

**Technology**
• Problem solving - e.g. how can a stick be attached to a stone to form an arrow or spear.  How can glue be made?  How do you build a house using only natural materials?

| The object(s) sketched, photographed, described in words | What this tells us about life in the past | Further ideas |
|---|---|---|
|  |  |  |

THE GNEISS, WHICH THE STONES ARE MADE OF, POSSIBLY CAME FROM THE HILLS IMMEDIATELY TO THE EAST WHERE SIMILAR STONES LIE ON THE SURFACE.

# Abbeys and Churches

## Changing beliefs

Many of the historic sites and monuments which survive today point to the central part played by religion in the lives of people in the past. Prehistoric burial sites, carved symbol stones and medieval abbeys for example provide a context for developing the themes of changing beliefs and the importance of certain places, rites and ceremonies. Christian belief can be traced from early crosses and cross-shaped carvings through abbeys, cathedrals and churches right up to the present day. The study of buildings and evidence from the past offers a tangible and intelligible way into the study of changing beliefs.

### The founding of abbeys

Many of the abbeys in Scotland were established during the reign of David I (1124-1153). This policy formed part of David I's efforts to reorganise Scottish society and guide his country into the faith and way of life of much of Western Europe. A more effective network of dioceses and parishes was created too, which led to cathedral and church building on quite a large scale. The building of monasteries formed an especially lavish part of David I's policy.

The king granted lands to abbeys like Kelso, Melrose and Dunfermline. Other wealthy people copied his example and by the end of his reign there were no less than 14 abbeys or priories.

### Religious orders

There were a number of different religious orders of monks, canons and friars in Scotland during the middle ages. Most of the monks looked back

RUTHWELL CROSS (NEAR DUMFRIES)

to St Benedict who had drawn up detailed rules for the lives of those who chose to devote their entire existence to God. All who entered

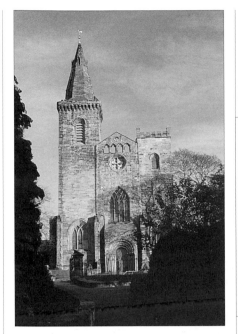

DUNFERMLINE ABBEY (FIFE)

abbeys, priories and nunneries had to give up all their worldly goods, to remain celibate and to obey the rules of the order. For example, there was supposed to be only one room with a fire in it and monks were to eat only the very simplest of vegetarian food. The actual implementation of these general rules, however, varied between orders.

Each order looked back to the particular founder who developed a particular approach in his religious house. The Cluniac Order, for example, which had abbeys at Paisley and Crossraguel, believed it right to offer God the best of human endeavour and their services became increasingly elaborate and their buildings more and more opulent. In contrast the Cistercians, who established several abbeys in Scotland, including one at Melrose, sought to live a far more simple life. The colour of the undyed habit that the Cistercians wore earned them the name of 'white monks'. The Augustinian canons at Jedburgh abbey followed rules thought to have been devised by St Augustine of Hippo. Their dress earned them the name of 'black canons'. Being canons meant that most of the brothers were fully trained priests who could thus celebrate the most important service, known as the 'mass'. They were also able to take the services in ordinary parish churches.

## Services

Abbeys were first and foremost centres of worship. Religious services called the 'hours' dominated the community's day.

| Service | Time (approximate) |
|---------|------|
| Matins | 3.30 |
| Prime | 6.00 |
| Terce | 7.30 |
| Sext | 11.30 |
| None | 2.30 |
| Vespers | 6.00 |
| Compline | 8.30 |

## Organisation of an abbey

Running an abbey was a demanding business that involved a range of specialists. Personnel varied from abbey to abbey but most monastic communities would have the following people :

**Abbot** – He was in overall charge, led the services, decided on punishments. He often eventually had his own house even though he was supposed to live with his monks.

**Prior** – He was the abbot's deputy.
**Novice Master** – He looked after the training of new recruits. They spent a year in the abbey before making their final decision to join the order.
**Sacrist** – He was in charge of items used in services such as silverware, candles and cloths, as well as ringing the bell to call the community to services.
**Cellarer** – He looked after the abbey's provisions and also helped to manage the lands belonging to the monastery.
**Almoner** – He cared for the poor who came to the abbey for help and looked after guests.
**Infirmarian** – He visited the sick and cared for community members who became unwell and were moved to the abbey's infirmary.

Abbey communities were led by able and educated people and it is not surprising that they were very successful at developing their estates, farming profitably and establishing or improving crafts like milling and sheep rearing. Some communities required their members to engage in a great deal of work ; others, like the Cistercians, recruited uneducated 'lay' brothers to carry out manual work, insisting that they attend only two of the many church services.

AUGUSTINIAN CANON

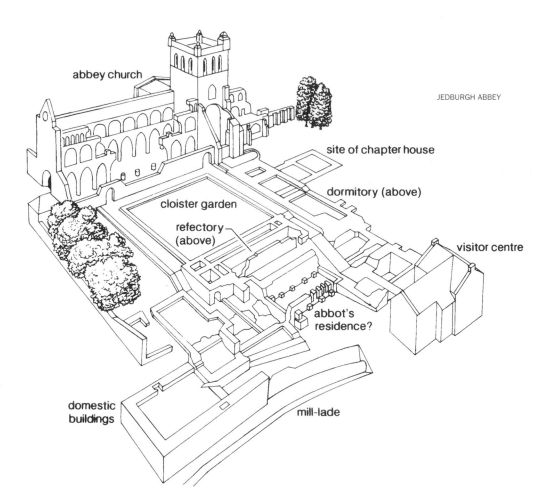

abbey church

JEDBURGH ABBEY

site of chapter house

dormitory (above)

cloister garden

refectory (above)

visitor centre

abbot's residence?

domestic buildings

mill-lade

## The layout of abbeys

The layout of most abbeys followed the same basic pattern. The abbey church would lie on an east-west axis and other buildings would be placed around a cloister area which was used for exercise and meditation. Abbeys were massive buildings that took perhaps 20 or even 50 years to complete. They also needed to be maintained,

A site visit involves reconstructing in children's minds the original condition of what are now ruined remains. The border abbeys were very vulnerable to assault from English armies and suffered on several occasions. With the coming of the Reformation to Scotland in the mid-16th century, abbeys became liable to attack from Protestants and, since most church buildings were no longer suitable for the new form of worship, these buildings fell from use and were no longer maintained. Often in the vicinity of a ruined abbey we can find

houses where the stone has been reused.

The ruined remains of great abbeys provide us with an insight into the importance and nature of religious belief in medieval times. The case study in this section focuses on Jedburgh Abbey, but as in other sections of this book the approach suggested would be appropriate at many religious sites throughout Scotland.

## Recommended reading
### For teachers
Guidebooks to individual Abbeys and Priories, Historic Scotland
C Cooksey : *Using Abbeys*, English Heritage 1992
R Fawcett : *Scottish Medieval Churches*, HMSO 1985
R Fawcett : *Scottish Abbeys and Priories*, Batsford / Historic Scotland 1994

### For pupils
FICTION
P Lively : *The Stained Glass Window*, Abelard-Schuman 1976
A child revisits medieval times through imagining a stained glass window coming to life.
R Sutcliffe : *The Witch's Brat*, OUP 1970
A child finds refuge in an abbey and then travels to London to help build a priory.

NON-FICTION
A Erskine and A Davison : *Scotland, at Peace, at War, 1263-1329*, Edward Arnold 1978
General background material on Scotland around the time many abbeys were built.
M Reeves : *The Medieval Monastery*, Then and There Series, Longman 1988

INCHCOLM ABBEY

## Some abbeys and priories in the care of Historic Scotland

**Arbroath Abbey**. Founded by King William the Lion in 1178. Parts of the abbey church and domestic buildings remain, notably the gatehouse range and the abbot's house. Site of the famous 'Declaration' of 1320.

**Crossraguel Abbey**, near Maybole. Cluniac abbey founded in the early 13th century by the Earl of Carrick. Interesting remains of church, cloister, chapter house and domestic premises. Fascinating drainage system.

**Dryburgh Abbey**, Borders. The ruins of this medieval abbey are remarkably complete.

**Inchcolm Abbey**, Firth of Forth. The best-preserved group of monastic buildings in Scotland. Reached by ferry from North Queensferry and South Queensferry.

**Inchmahome Priory,** Lake of Menteith. Augustinian priory founded in 1238. Reached by ferry.

**Melrose Abbey**, Borders. Founded around 1136 as a Cistercian Abbey by David I.

INCHMAHOME PRIORY

JEDBURGH ABBEY

## Jedburgh Abbey

Jedburgh Abbey was founded as a priory in 1138 and raised to abbey status in 1154. The black-robed canons here belonged to the Augustinian order. The key features of the site are the substantial remains of the mainly 12th-century church and the fragmentary foundations of the canons' domestic buildings. The site of a mill lade can be identified and the herb garden has been developed to include the types of plants which would have featured during the middle ages.

A School Pack for Jedburgh Abbey containing slides and activity sheets has been prepared for teachers, and there is also a video about the abbey and its inhabitants which can be viewed on site or borrowed for use in schools.

## Making the most of a visit

PREPARATION

Before visiting it would be helpful if pupils
• know about King David I and his beliefs, and why he wanted to found abbeys
• understand the importance of the Christian faith to people of the period
• have studied pictures of abbeys and built up the appropriate vocabulary to label the different buildings
• have looked at the different members of an abbey community
• have studied an appropriate map to discuss the location of the abbey
• have practised estimating and measuring skills
• have become competent in using and drafting a plan of a group of buildings

ON-SITE ACTIVITIES

As with other sites, the visit to an abbey could involve pupils looking at the site, the range of buildings and their use. They could create a picture of what it would have been like to live there by comparing sights and sounds of the past with those of today. Alternatively one particular part of the site such as the abbey church or the herb garden could provide the focus for activities.

Three examples of activities are provided here – Different Points of View, The Missing Pieces and What, Where and When.

## Different points of view

### A MONK'S VIEW

Pupils imagine themselves as a medieval canon who is taking a newly arrived guest on a tour of the abbey. Where will the guest need to be taken? What will the guest need to know?

### A GHOST'S VIEW

A medieval monk returns to the present day. What can be seen that he can remember? What has changed? What sights and sounds did he experience and how do they compare with those he can see and hear today?

### A FILM-MAKER'S VIEW

Pupils adopt the role of a film-maker with a commission to shoot a film about the abbey. Visually attractive locations will be needed. Photographs and sketches will have to be made to plan the project. A sequence will be required and the different locations will therefore have to be marked on a plan.

### A MASTER MASON'S REPORT

Pupils imagine that they are the master-mason showing the completed abbey to a wealthy benefactor. The choice of location, placing and range of buildings and the grandeur of the finished abbey should all be considered. Pupils should also see that design is more than just looking good. A symmetrical design for example strengthens the structure of the building as well as being pleasing to the eye. Pupils should use a map, plan and measuring tape.

### A BUSINESSMAN'S VIEW

Pupils adopt the role of someone brought in to report on how the abbey makes money today. Pupils should look at entrance charges, goods for sale in the shop and other ways that money is made. Pupils have to write a report on what could be done on the site to attract more visitors and make more money without ruining the abbey.

Each of these roles will need a guidance sheet which explains
• the role to be adopted
• resources to use

# The Missing Pieces

In this exercise you will find drawings of parts of the abbey. But each drawing has some important bits missing.

You must find each part shown in the drawings by walking around. Then you have to sketch in the missing parts of each drawing.

You must also mark where each part is on your site plan. Each drawing has a number, so enter that number in the correct position on your site plan.

### Remember! the drawings have more than one bit missing

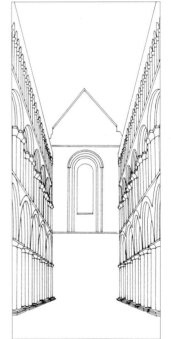

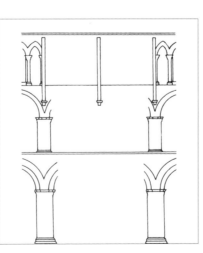

# What, Where and When

In this exercise, you can see pictures of the daily life of the CANONS of Jedburgh Abbey.
You must find out WHAT they are doing, WHERE they are in the abbey and WHEN during the day it would be.
You must also mark where each place is on your site plan, using the number of each picture.
You will find the information you need around the site and in the interpretation room in the visitor centre.

**1**
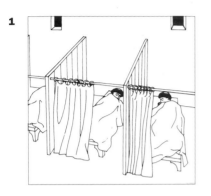

WHAT
Here the canons are _____
_____

WHERE
This part of the abbey is called the
_____

WHEN
The canons do this between
_____ and _____

**5**

**2**

WHAT
Here the canons are _____

WHERE
This part of the abbey is called the
_____

**6**

**3**

WHAT
Here the canons are _____
_____

WHERE
This part of the abbey is called the
_____

WHEN
The canons do this between _____
and _____

**7**

**4**

WHAT
Here the canons are _____
_____

WHERE
This part of the abbey is called the
_____

WHEN
The canons do this between _____
and _____

**8**

WHAT

Here the canons are _____

_____

WHERE

This part of the abbey is called the

_____

WHEN

The canons do this at _____

and _____ and _____ and _____

and _____ and _____ and _____

and _____

WHAT

Here the canons are _____

_____

WHERE

This part of the abbey is called the

_____

WHEN

The canons do this at _____

and _____ and between _____

_____ and _____

WHAT

Here the canons are _____

_____

WHERE

This part of the abbey is called the

_____

WHAT

Here the canons are _____

_____

WHERE

This part of the abbey is called the

_____

## Following up fieldwork

UNDERSTANDING PEOPLE IN THE PAST

• Time and sequence can be established by plotting a time line (using the correct terminology) for the establishment, life-span and end of the Abbey's active use as a religious site. These events can be noted against those wider events that explain the abbey's fortunes.

• Pupils could be provided with a series of pictures taken at the site and asked to conclude what they can from each. This could lead to a discussion about evidence from the past.

• Pupils are encouraged to consider the 'whys' of past life and events. Why would men wish to live such a life? How did this lifestyle decide the type of building they needed? How did the coming of the abbey change life in the area?

UNDERSTANDING PEOPLE AND PLACE

• Pupils could create a large wall map/plan of the site, using colour coding. Reasons for settlement growth in this location can be noted.

SCIENCE AND TECHNOLOGY

• Writing – experimenting with quill pen and ink.

• Lighting – the problem of lighting the abbey could lead to candle-making.

• Lifting weights – the problems involved in lifting heavy blocks of stone could lead to work with pulleys and weights.

• Telling the time – after considering how the canons told the time for their many services, a sand-timer could be made using two bottles and a card insert between them with experiments to vary hole diameter to modify sand flow.

• Growing of herbs and discussion of their various uses in the past and today.

EXPRESSIVE ARTS

• Role play e.g. 'A novice master interviews a would-be entrant to the abbey.'

• Using shoe boxes to create a model/diorama of the abbey.

• Using pens and paints to recreate an illuminated manuscript.

• Making a stained glass window from coloured paper.

• Making a collage showing figures at work and prayer.

• Making a poster to encourage visitors to come to the abbey.

• Listening to music of the period.

ENGLISH LANGUAGE

• Scripting and recording a video recording of a visit to the abbey using sound effects like bells and music. (Several visits may be necessary.)

• Creating a simple guide book written for 7 to 8 year olds.

• Working out and writing up the 'Abbey Rules.'

# Castles and Forts

During the 12th century, individuals who had been granted control of areas on behalf of the king, built castles for their administrative centres. Symbols of lordship to impress those under the jurisdiction of their owners, these castles also provided a defence against enemies.

Gradually castles developed from the early wooden towers built on a natural or artificial motte to prestigious buildings of stone reflecting the importance, power and wealth of their owners as well as providing them with defences should the need arise. In response to the increasing sophistication of attacking methods and siege machines, high curtain walls and other features were introduced.

Although royal palaces such as Linlithgow, Stirling and Edinburgh continued to expand during the later middle ages, by the end of the 15th century there had been a move towards the more compact form of the tower-house, one of the earliest being that built by Archibald the Grim at Threave about 1370. Nowadays when we look at the tower-houses we are tempted to believe that they were self-contained but there is plenty of archaeological evidence to show that there would have been very many additional buildings - often including the great hall and kitchen - built in a courtyard known as a 'barmkin' which surrounded the tower-house. The tower-house provided the lord with more privacy than the earlier castles in which living accommodation was shared with servants and retainers.

During the more settled times of the late 16th and early 17th century, the focus moves even further from defence to comfort. In some cases, as at Dirleton and Caerlaverock, for example, separate buildings were erected with great attention paid to symmetry in design and decorative carvings. Formal gardens and summerhouses were also a feature of these more confident times.

Most castles have evidence of development over a long period of time and although this may make initial understanding more difficult, recognising the features of the different phases in building adds much to the interest of the monument and provides a practical introduction to interpretation of evidence from the past.

If a castle which often covers a large site is to be the focus for fieldwork, a useful approach is to give all pupils an overview of main features of the site before they pursue their particular line of enquiry. This could be done through

• group discussion in response to adult questions. (In some cases School Packs provide an 'Orientation Tour' card with questions and answers)
• completion of a map/plan/diagram
• completion of an introductory activity sheet that breaks down an aspect into a series of short response tasks

In all cases it is important to encourage the pupils to collect evidence, evaluate and interpret it and to record their findings in a variety of ways. The degree to which work is carried out by pupils speaking, writing, sketching, or using drama, must be up to the individual teacher who must also decide the extent and level of demand of the tasks set.

There are a number of questions which pupils could consider on visiting any castle site. Although similar to those asked in the previous chapter, there are a few which are specific to this type of site.

**DUNADD FORT** (ARGYLL) – ONE OF THE SITES USED BY THE KING OF THE SCOTS BETWEEN THE 7TH AND 9TH CENTURIES. ARCHAEOLOGICAL EVIDENCE HAS SHOWN THAT THIS MUST HAVE BEEN AN IMPRESSIVE STRUCTURE. ARTEFACTS DISCOVERED ON SITE INCLUDED FINE JEWELLERY AND PIECES OF POTTERY WHICH ORIGINATED IN FRANCE.

**DUFFUS CASTLE** (NEAR ELGIN) – THIS IS THE BEST SURVIVING EXAMPLE OF A MOTTE AND BAILEY CASTLE IN THE CARE OF HISTORIC SCOTLAND. ALTHOUGH THE STONE STRUCTURE DATES FROM THE 14TH CENTURY , ARCHAEOLOGICAL EXCAVATION HAS SHOWN THAT THIS WAS THE SITE OF A WOODEN FORTIFICATION BUILT ABOUT 1150 FOR THE LORD WHO WAS GRANTED THE LAND BY KING DAVID 1.

How long did this castle take to build? What building materials were used? How does the building reflect the time, wealth and building skill available when it was constructed?

Who lived in this castle? What sort of home did the castle provide for the people who lived in it? What evidence is there for cooking methods, eating and sleeping arrangements, storage facilities?

What kind of weapons and tactics would attackers use when this castle was first built? Have the defences of the castle been altered to defend against more sophisticated weapons such as cannons and guns?

Who looks after this castle today? How many visitors are there each year and where do they come from? How could a visit to this castle be made more interesting for visitors? Do visitors damage this site?

Many of the questions given here could be built into a 'trail booklet' if it is felt that pupils could cope with all that is involved. Bothwell Castle is sufficiently compact for this to be feasible but some sites will be far too large. Each group will need a good-sized plan with numbered stopping places marked on it which correspond to their activity sheets. Material on such sheets needs to be well spaced out and should require the pupils to look carefully and to think about the evidence before them.

Children could be given a specific task for which evidence is required that calls for accurate measuring and recording. For example such a task could be 'You have been asked to make a scale model of _____ Castle to be placed in the local tourist office. You will need to make sketches, take photographs, record measurements and add notes to your plan to help you prepare for this task.'

Three different types of castle have been chosen as case studies for this section : *Bothwell Castle*, a fine example of a medieval castle which was involved in the wars with England of the late 13th and 14th centuries ; *Edzell Castle*, a building which was developed through several stages to a fine mansion house with a beautiful renaissance garden ; and *Fort George*, a military fort begun in 1748 in response to the Jacobite threat and still in use today as a barracks. As well as

reflecting three different periods from the time line each case study focuses on a different approach in terms of skills and types of investigation. In many cases these approaches are interchangeable and may easily be adapted to suit other castle sites.

## Recommended reading

**Useful reference books for teachers**
Official Guides to individual sites, Historic Scotland
T Copeland : *A Teacher's Guide to Using Castles*, English Heritage 1994
C Tabraham : *Scottish Castles and Fortifications*, HMSO 1990

**Fiction for pupils**
D K Broster : *The Flight of the Heron*, Heinemann 1970
Set in Scotland during the 1745 uprising.
F M Hendry : *Quest for a Babe*, Canongate 1990
Adventures of the Clan Maclean set in 16th-century Scotland.
F M Hendry : *Quest for a Kelpie*, Canongate 1986
Set around Nairn during the 1745 uprising.
M Hunter : *You Never Knew Her As I Did*, Hamish Hamilton 1981
The imprisonment and escape of Queen Mary from Loch Leven Castle seen through the eyes of a young page.

**Non-fiction for pupils**
B Davison : *Looking at a Castle*, Kingfisher 1987
E Dunlop and A Kamm : *Scottish Homes through the Ages*, R Drew 1985
Especially useful for younger children.
G Jarvie : *Scottish Castles*, HMSO Scottie Books 1995
With lots of colour illustrations and follow-up activities for children of 8 - 12.
R Mathews : *Building a Castle, Living in a Castle, Siege*. Firefly books 1990
J Robottom : *Castles and Cathedrals*, Longman
R Unstead : *See Inside a Castle*, Usborne 1982

**THREAVE CASTLE** (DUMFRIES AND GALLOWAY) – BUILT ABOUT 1370. ALTHOUGH IT LOOKS A SOLITARY TOWER, NUMEROUS ADDITIONAL BUILDINGS WOULD HAVE STOOD IN A SURROUNDING 'BARMKIN' OR COURTYARD.

# Features of a Medieval Castle

**KITCHEN** - DOUNE CASTLE SCHOOL PACK

**CROSS SECTION OF A TOWER-HOUSE**
SMAILHOLM TOWER SCHOOL PACK

**LORD'S TABLE** - DOUNE CASTLE SCHOOL PACK

CAERLAVEROCK CASTLE

## Some castles and forts to visit

**Caerlaverock Castle**, 8 miles SE of Dumfries. Fine example of a medieval castle with surrounding water-filled moat.

**Craigmillar Castle**, Edinburgh. Most of the remains date from the 15th and 16th centuries. There are many rooms to explore.

**Dirleton Castle,** East Lothian. The oldest part of this castle dates from the 13th century. This castle has very interesting gardens.

**Doune Castle**, near Stirling. Impressive 14th-century castle built for the Regent Albany.

**Dunstaffnage Castle**, near Oban. An impressive 13th-century castle with a great curtain wall, built on a rock.

**Huntingtower Castle**, near Perth. Two fine and complete towers, one of the 15th-16th century and the other of 16th-century origin linked by a 17th century range. There are fine painted ceilings in this castle.

**Huntly Castle**. Dating from 16th and 17th centuries. Interesting carvings.

**Stirling Castle**. Impressive castle in a wonderful setting. Associations with many kings and queens of Scotland, including James IV, James V and James VI. Interpretative displays.

**Tantallon Castle**, East Lothian. An impressive castle site, built on a promontory. Views of the Bass Rock.

VIEW OF BOTHWELL CASTLE OVERLOOKING THE RIVER CLYDE

## Bothwell Castle

The ruins of Bothwell Castle manage to convey even today the sense of power and prestige which must have impressed those who saw it during the middle ages. A visit to this castle, which changed hands several times during the wars with England of the 13th and 14th centuries, provides a marvellous opportunity for pupils to investigate aspects of medieval warfare.

Whilst many events can be linked to the castle, two sieges in particular are worth considering. In 1298 the Scots began a siege of the castle which was to last 14 months until eventually through lack of food the castle was taken. In contrast, Edward I's English army was able to recapture the castle in less than a month in September 1301. His key weapon was the belfry, a tall wooden siege tower fitted with a drawbridge, which allowed the soldiers to cross on to the top of the castle's defensive walls.

The 'donjon' is the main survivor from the 13th century, since much of the rest of the castle which survives

was developed in the late 14th and 15th centuries. The later additions of great hall and chapel provide a study of castle life in the middle ages. In order to avoid confusion, however, pupils should concentrate, at least initially, on the remains of one period or the other.

A mighty keep or 'donjon' was the first part to be built. It is this structure that was fought over in the first half of the 14th century, falling first to one side and then to the other.

The great curtain walls and additional towers were largely added in the late 14th and early 15th centuries.

THE BELFRY WAS TRUNDLED ALONG ON 30 WAGGONS, ASSEMBLED ON SITE AND ROLLED UP TO THE WALLS.

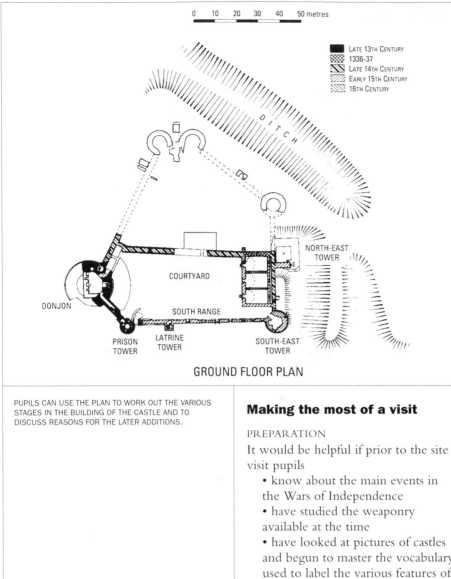

0  10  20  30  40  50 metres

■ LATE 13TH CENTURY
▨ 1336-37
▨ LATE 14TH CENTURY
▧ EARLY 15TH CENTURY
▨ 16TH CENTURY

DITCH

NORTH-EAST TOWER

COURTYARD

DONJON

SOUTH RANGE

PRISON TOWER   LATRINE TOWER   SOUTH-EAST TOWER

**GROUND FLOOR PLAN**

PUPILS CAN USE THE PLAN TO WORK OUT THE VARIOUS STAGES IN THE BUILDING OF THE CASTLE AND TO DISCUSS REASONS FOR THE LATER ADDITIONS.

## Making the most of a visit

PREPARATION

It would be helpful if prior to the site visit pupils
- know about the main events in the Wars of Independence
- have studied the weaponry available at the time
- have looked at pictures of castles and begun to master the vocabulary used to label the various features of castles
- have found the site on an appropriate map
- are familiar with plans as a way of

'DONJON'

presenting information
- are competent in handling measuring equipment

ON-SITE INVESTIGATIONS

**Why was the castle built here?**

The pupil would be encouraged to
- discuss the location of the castle in relation to the natural features of the area
- record the site of the castle on a provided map outline
- sketch/photograph the castle from different viewpoints

**How will it be best to defend the castle?**

This could be explored by a group of pupils who are preparing a report for the lord of the castle on what to do if the enemy tries a number of approaches.

**What was it like to live in the castle?**

Pupils are asked to consider what life was like for different groups of people at the castle such as the lord's family, servants, soldiers and perhaps even prisoners. They could be given a series of questions which asks them to consider the water supply, living and sleeping accommodation, lighting, latrines, stores, cooking arrangements and other accommodation which can be identified. They should consider not only sights but sounds and smells. They could also consider what different kinds of rubbish would have been produced in medieval times.

Historical fiction, storytelling on site, collaborative story-making that begins by setting the scene for an adventure, discussion of the sounds of the past, role play and discussion of what you would once have seen here, all help develop a sense of life in the past.

**What is the castle like now?**

This question asks the children to look closely at how the site is looked after today and the efforts which are made to help visitors. Children could also consider what improvements could be made to the site to make it more interesting for visitors. As these ideas are developed, children are encouraged to think what is special about the site and this can then lead on to a discussion of the meaning of heritage.

# Our Plan of Attack

My Lord,

You asked us to prepare a plan for attacking Bothwell Castle.  We had to look at all the possibilities before we handed in our report.

You asked us to think about

Are there any ways in which we can creep up close to the castle unseen?

Are there any sides of the castle that are quite impossible to attack?

Will it be easy to attack the towers?

Will any of the walls be easy to break through or climb over?

If we get into the courtyard will it be easy to capture the rest of the castle?

Will the enemy be able to shoot at us and pour things on us?

Should we try and tunnel under the walls?

We have decided it will be best to

_____

_____

for the following  reasons

1
_____

2
_____

3
_____

# Tourist Attraction

*Bothwell Castle*

Castles like Bothwell were built as homes and places of defence, not as tourist attractions. Any changes which are made to improve the castle for tourists must not damage or alter its character.

Make up a plan for improvements for visitors. Once you have decided what is needed, suggest where it should go and what problems you would have to consider.

Take notes on your visit so that you are able to write your report later.

**Here are some pictures to help you.**

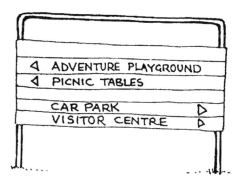

## Edzell Castle

Edzell Castle (6 miles north of Brechin) dates from the end of the 15th century and was extended and elaborated both in the later 16th century and again in 1604. Unlike the site of Bothwell Castle, the site for Edzell Castle was dominated by rising land which an enemy could easily exploit. But at this later period, a sheltered and sunny location mattered more than defensive features.

Edzell Castle is one of a number of castles built in this later period which provide evidence of a safer, more comfortable and elegant lifestyle. Features of the site provide insights into a changing way of life during the timespan defined in the 5-14 guidelines as 'Renaissance, Reformation and the Age of Discovery'.

Edzell Castle also offers an interesting example of a study over a period of time. An early medieval motte which is thought to have been the site of an original fortification built of wood can still be seen nearby. Pupils can therefore see evidence of the development of the castle from wooden tower on motte site to tower house to renaissance house.

The main features of the site are

- a later 15th-century L-plan tower house typical of the period, with gunloops to provide defence against the military technology of the time
- a later 16th-century range of buildings developed from 1553 to provide the owners, the Lindsay family, with a far more comfortable lifestyle
- a walled garden with summer house and bathhouse which was created in 1604 during the relatively peaceful reign of James VI.

The castle has links with important events and people in the past : Mary Queen of Scots held a Privy Council at Edzell on 25th August 1562 and the sale of the property to the York Building Company was a consequence of the then owner Lord Panmure's support for the Jacobites in the uprising of 1715.

GENERAL VIEW OF THE CASTLE AND GARDENS

### GARDENS

The theme of gardens in the past could be developed at Edzell. The formal style of the renaissance garden and the importance of gardens growing herbs and medicinal plants could be investigated. For younger children, the garden at Edzell offers a tremendous stimulus for exploring the five senses. During the summer months the gardener is able to provide a box planted with herbs for children to touch and take samples.

### DRAMA

The garden at Edzell provides a marvellous setting for the re-enactment of scenes which might have taken place during the 17th century. Pupils can imagine what it would have been like to have lived at that time from the point of view of the lord and also of the servant. Music from the period could be rehearsed beforehand and played on site. The arrival of a special visitor could form the focus of the drama. In many regions, drama specialists are pleased to advise on using a historic building in this way.

### ACTIVITIES AND INVESTIGATIONS

Pupils could be asked to prepare a guided tour either as a modern guide or as Sir David Lindsay.

*'You are Sir David Lindsay. It is the year 1605. Important guests have arrived. Take them on a tour of your castle and garden.*

*a) Mark on the plan all the places you will stop at.*

*b) Note down all that you will tell your guests at each stopping place.'*

DRAWING OF CARVING IN GARDEN WALL

# Edzell Castle

*Can you complete this drawing?*

*Which of these masons' marks can you find?*

*Put a tick beside the picture of any bird which you see*

HOUSE MARTIN

SWALLOW

PHEASANT

ROBIN

SPARROW

WOOD PIGEON

DVM SPIRO SPERO

S DL

D IF

1604

*Tick the box every time you see this coat of arms*

# Edzell Castle

*Look for clues in the castle and gardens
to help you find the missing words.*

Latin words in the hedge which
mean 'while I breathe I hope'        _ _ _ S _ _ _ _  _ _ _ _ _

Flower of Scotland in the garden hedge        _ _ I _ _ _ _

The oldest part of the castle        _ _ _ _ R

Where you find wooden shutters        _ _ _ D _ _ _

Another name for the toilet        _ A _ _ _ _ _

They would carry food from the
kitchen to the hall        _ _ _ V _ _ _ _

We look after Edzell Castle        _ _ _ _ _ _ I _ _ _ _ _ _ _ _ _

A special oven was needed to bake this        _ _ _ _ D

Guns might have been fired from these        _ _ _ _ _ _ L _ _

Initials on the carving of Mars        I _

These birds especially like to nest
in the garden wall        _ _ _ _ _  _ _ _ _ _ N _

The lady with the bird on her head        D _ _ _ _ _ _ _ _ _

A lovely house in the garden        _ _ _ _ _ _ _ _ _ S _

Type of wood used for panelling        _ A _

She held a meeting at Edzell
Castle in 1562        _ _ _ Y _ _ _ _ _ _ _ _ _ _ _ _

Show the custodian your answers and you will win a sticker

HISTORIC SCOTLAND

AERIAL VIEW OF FORT

## Fort George

At Ardersier near Inverness lies one of the finest examples of 18th-century military architecture to be found in Europe. Fort George took over 20 years to construct and cost the then-awesome amount of £200,000 (more than a billion pounds today).

The study of Fort George forms a vital part of studies located in the 'Age of Revolutions' timespan as defined in the 5-14 Environmental Studies guidelines; for it provides first-hand evidence of the Jacobite Risings and the government's struggle to open up and control the Highlands. Fort George provides the finest of all the reminders on the landscape of the Hanoverian government's fear of the Jacobites.

The scale and design of Fort George and the weaponry to be found on it illustrate the degree to which military technology evolved during the late 18th century. Its walls were designed by General William Skinner and constructed under the supervision of the famous Adam family of architects and master masons. The walls were intended to resist the shot of powerful cannon and musketry.

Since the fort has been in continuous use as a military base and has not suffered from military action, it provides a very full picture of military life in the past and offers potential for the development of the theme of military life across time. During the later 18th and 19th centuries, the fort became the centre for the raising of Highland regiments for service overseas and the Regimental Museum of the Queen's Own Highlanders, which is independently run, has a very interesting display of weapons and exhibitions which extend beyond the 18th century.

WAS FORT GEORGE WELL DESIGNED? Pupils might pretend that they were spies. They could be directed to consider

- the different parts that make up the overall system of outer defensive walls.
- the ditch and the use of drawbridges. ( Note that the defensive ditch on the landward side can be flooded at high tide.)
- the sheer width of the walls and their construction.
- the angled shapes and the reasons for this.

The sheer scale of the walls means that estimating height and pacing will be necessary since accurate measuring is not feasible.

WHAT WAS IT LIKE TO BE A SOLDIER AT FORT GEORGE?

This involves exploring the barracks, the well, the reconstructed barrackrooms, watching the video and visiting the chapel. The reconstructed barrackrooms allow pupils to compare rooms of different periods, to look for change and to compare accommodation for different ranks. The evidence here could be recorded by providing a partially completed letter home from the room occupant with spaces left for the insertion of items that pupils are asked to locate. Pupils could also fill in a table like the one below as they gather evidence from different sources.

PUPILS CAN VIEW RECONSTRUCTIONS OF BARRACKS FROM THE 18TH CENTURY AND THERE IS ALSO A VIDEO ON SITE WHICH LOOKS AT THE LIVES OF SOLDIERS WHO HAVE LIVED ON THIS SITE FROM THE 18TH CENTURY TO THE PRESENT DAY.

|  | *Private John Anderson 1780* | *Private George Moffat 1868* |
|---|---|---|
| *number of people to a room* |  |  |
| *number and types of beds* |  |  |
| *lighting used* |  |  |
| *fuel used for heating* |  |  |

HOW IS THE FORT USED TODAY?

How does the fact that Fort George is still used as an army base affect the site as a visitor attraction? How is living at Fort George which is a tourist attraction different from other army barracks? How does the presence of the army help to preserve the site? (Through heating the rooms and general maintenance.) What items are sold in the shop? Do they have any links with the site?

**Preparation**

A background knowledge of the Jacobites in general and the '45 in particular is essential. It will be helpful to look at the location of forts and barracks and the military road network in relation to Fort George. Pupils should know something of the military technology of the time.

Fort George is an exposed location and warm clothing, waterproof garments, and clipboards to which paper can be firmly attached are essential.

A School Pack with activity sheets linked to 5–14 has been produced and teachers may wish to obtain this either from the Education Officer or directly from Fort George several weeks before visiting.

The sheer size of the Fort must be taken into account when planning activities with the pupils. If possible the site should be visited several times so that the pupils can pick up where they left off. If only one visit is possible or time is limited, it is better that pupils concentrate on one question or issue.

ROTHESAY CASTLE

# Follow-up work

### UNDERSTANDING PEOPLE IN THE PAST

• Further research into a people's lives and events of the period being studied.
• Discussion about whether the site should be knocked down and modern housing put up in its place.

### UNDERSTANDING PEOPLE AND PLACE

Pupils could create a large-scale plan to show how the castle has made good use of its site and how it developed over time.

Pupils could consider the effect the castle had on the surrounding area in the past and compare that with its 20th-century role as a tourist attraction.

The location of the castle on a map of the wider area could be labelled to show its significance in terms of communications, etc.

### MATHEMATICS

Information gathered during fieldwork can be transferred and recorded on suitable plans and cross-sections. Data like wall thickness and the location of windows big enough to climb through, angles of fire from arrow slits and gun loops may also play a part in any work relating to accounts of attack and defence.

Plotting the shape of Fort George or a section of a castle accurately and measuring and recording angles of fire are a practical focus for work in mathematics. Statistics showing visitors and their nationality can be shown in graph form.

### EXPRESSIVE ARTS

Possibilities include the construction of a collage of weapons, the making of a figure of a soldier or a lady decorated in suitable materials, the design of a shield and its coat of arms or the planning and creation of a large scene such as an attack on the castle.

Pupils can create a poster encouraging people to visit the site.

The splendid uniforms of soldiers in the 18th century could be recreated in 2- or 3-dimensional form using a range of materials following a visit to Fort George.

### DRAMA

Drama can be used on site or as part of the follow-up work. Following a visit to a medieval castle pupils might prepare a medieval feast with entertainers. Data gathered at Fort George should help pupils prepare scenes such as

• an officer interviewing a soldier guilty of a minor offence and sentencing him
• A general coming on a tour of inspection and interviewing a range of soldiers about their lives
• A drill sergeant training his men.

### ENGLISH LANGUAGE

Both functional and imaginative writing can be developed as pupils record their visit and create 'documents' such as : a spy's report, a letter from a prisoner pleading for rescue, the menu for a feast, words to describe the castle pinned on a castle shape. Pupils can also give a short talk to the rest of the group on an aspect of the visit.

• Pupils can write letters to the custodian thanking him or her for the visit.
• Pupils can produce a script for slides taken during the visit.
Following a visit to Fort George pupils

DUNSTAFFNAGE CASTLE – GENERAL VIEW

could produce
• A soldier's letter home from a lonely posting
• Orders to soldiers drafted as notices for the walls
• A speech for William Skinner to give to the official gathering to celebrate the completion of the Fort.

### SCIENCE AND TECHNOLOGY

Medieval warfare provides a context for the exploration of issues such as making a missile-firing machine and considering questions of weights, levers, trajectories. Pupils can also draw up plans for making a siege tower. They can test structures of different designs to test for strength in terms of being able to bear a load using a guidance sheet with instructions such as 'King Edward I wishes you to build him a giant siege tower. He wishes you to think about these questions...'

Pupils might consider how to project a missile to cause damage at short and at long range and find out why barrel length and width makes a difference.

Pupils might investigate different ways of colouring cloth.

Pupils can carry out controlled experiments to investigate materials and structures which are capable of resisting heat.

Following a visit to a castle with a garden such as Edzell, pupils might look at the many uses of plants and herbs in the past and today.

Pupils can look at the different means used in the past to provide heating and lighting.

**CRICHTON CASTLE** – THE ITALIAN FACADE

# Industrial Sites

The activities involved in crafts are as old as human settlement itself and begin with prehistoric craftsmen who once developed skills in flint-knapping and tool construction. For much of human history it was human muscle that powered any equipment that was used but by medieval times the harnessing of wind and water power was well established in enterprises that were commonly on quite a small scale. The transport revolution and the growth of urban population made possible larger production units and the emergence of factory-scale operations, notably at first in late 18th-century textiles. Steam power added to the process, freeing factory owners from the need to locate their buildings beside a suitable river and the process of applying power to production is a story that then moves with accelerating speed.

Crafts and industries may be explored to shed light on life at a

BONAWE IRONWORKS, ARGYLL.

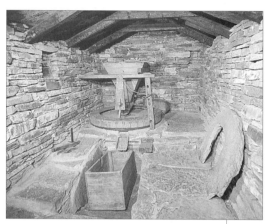

DOUNBY CLICK MILL, ORKNEY.

DALLAS DHU DISTILLERY, MORAY.

particular time, or they may also be pursued through a sweep of time. The purpose of the study may be primarily historical, or it may equally have a geographical or scientific purpose as its chief driving force. Crafts and industries not only provide evidence of past life and how it changed over time, but also show how science and technology have been developed to meet human needs. A visit to an industrial site prompts consideration of the effects of industry on the environment and leads to consideration of the advantages and disadvantages of industrial progress and the effects this has on the environment.

In this section the focus is on New Abbey Corn Mill, near Dumfries. It is hoped that the ideas given here will be adapted and used at other industrial sites whether or not they are in the care of Historic Scotland.

## Recommended reading

**For teachers**
Official guides to sites, Historic Scotland

**For pupils**
K Fidler : *The desperate journey*, Canongate 1984
Part of the journey is located in an 18th-century Glasgow mill.
A Schlee : *Ask me no questions*, Macmillan 1976
Two children live next door to a school in 1847 in London and discover that children taken from a workhouse to learn a trade live here.
R Swindells : *A candle in the dark*, Swift 1987
Jimmy leaves the workhouse for the colliery.

*Wheels at Work*, Wayland 1994
Part of series focusing on how things work. Reading age 9-11.

## New Abbey Corn Mill

New Abbey Corn Mill dates from the later 18th century but is located on a far more ancient mill site. Close by the mill today lie the remains of Sweetheart Abbey, a clue to the existence as early perhaps as the 14th century of a mill on this site for grinding oats to provide food for the abbey's inhabitants.

In a land as wet and hilly as Scotland, the use of waterpower to drive a range of machinery is a well-established feature of life from the middle ages. Even today in the midst of urban areas it is possible to find the word 'mill' in a street name marking the former presence of water-powered machinery that has now vanished.

Waterpower has to be carefully managed and New Abbey Corn Mill provides a good illustration of all that was involved. Water had to be drawn off a river or a burn but siting the mill directly on such a flow of water was not sensible since the height and speed of water could not be controlled. A system of sluice gates was needed which, when opened, allowed water to flow down a channel, or 'lade', to the wheel. The speed of the wheel could be varied by altering the volume of water flowing down the lade. Wheel design varied and could be of breastshot, undershot, overshot or pitch-back pattern, the latter being used at New Abbey Mill. After serving its purpose the water had to be guided back to rejoin the river from which it originally came.

Gearing machines were needed to transmit the power from the slowly spinning drive wheel to the machinery housed inside. This gearing served to alter the speed and angle of drive.

A watermill therefore had a significant impact on the local environment, for millers often built weirs across rivers to keep a steady height of water for entry to the lade; and many millers also created millponds to act as reservoirs of power. Both of these constructions altered the habitat for wildlife. Moreover, a mill was a focus for traffic in the vicinity of the river. A ford or bridge would be needed at the river and routes to and from the mill would gradually develop. Sometimes a whole settlement (a 'milltown' or 'milton') emerged nearby. In the case of New Abbey, however, we must also consider the impact that Sweetheart Abbey had on settlement growth.

A VIDEO PRESENTATION 'THE MILLER'S TALE' GIVES AN INTERESTING HISTORY OF THE MILL AND THE SURROUNDING AREA. THIS MAY BE VIEWED ON SITE OR BORROWED BY TEACHERS PRIOR TO VISITING.

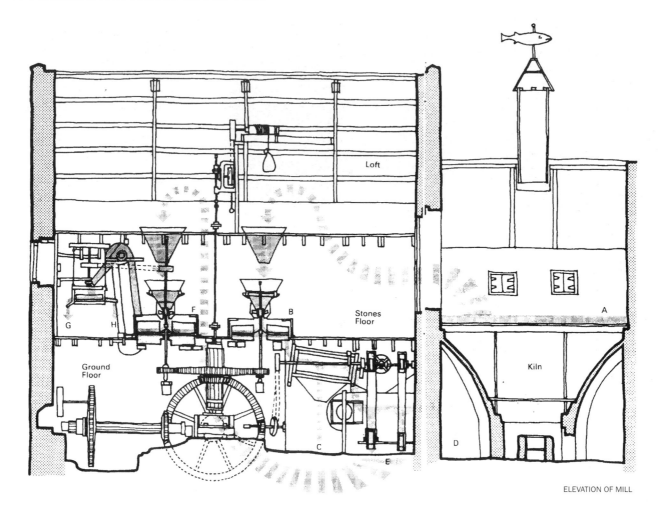

ELEVATION OF MILL

### The Grain Flow

The newly dried grain (A) was fed into the shelling stones (B). Afterwards, the dust (C) and husks (D) were removed in the boulting machine and fan. The clean and shelled grain (E) passed through the finishing stones (F) and then to the shaking sieve, where the over-sized grains (G) were separated from the finished meal (H).

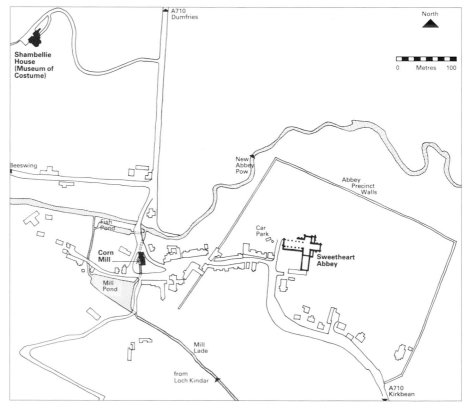

PLAN OF THE MILL AND THE SURROUNDING AREA.

NEW ABBEY MILL POND

## Making the most of a visit

PREPARATION
Before visiting the site it would be helpful if pupils
• understood the importance of the location of the mill
• had thought about the ways in which water can be used to drive machinery
• had knowledge of the whole sequence involved from planting grain to cooking the oatmeal that has been ground at a mill
• were aware of the terminology used to describe mill features such as sluice, lade, kiln, bed stone
• had studied aspects of rural life in the later 18th and 19th centuries including travel, ways of cooking, the importance of oatmeal in the diet and the localised scale for manufacturing.
• were warned of the dangers on a site where there is water and working machinery.

ON-SITE ACTIVITIES AND INVESTIGATIONS
**Why has this site been chosen for the mill and how has it been altered because of the mill?**

Using either a provided outline map, or a sketch map that they have made themselves, pupils should be asked to imagine that they are surveyors and that their task is to record
- the distance of the mill from its power source of water
- an impression of the fall in height from this source to the mill
- the location of the mill pond in relation to the mill
- the overall layout of the mill buildings
- the road system serving the mill
- any bridges in the area
- any additional buildings close by, other than the mill itself; and the use of such buildings.

## How is the water flow controlled and managed?

This will involve measuring and recording activities that are best plotted on a large outline site plan to which details can be added in note form. In addition, photographs and/or sketches of key feature would be useful. Again, the investigation could be broken up into a series of questions.
- How is the flow of water into the lade controlled?
  - How long is the lade
    a) from point of entry to the mill pond?
    b) from the pond to the wheel?
    c) from the wheel to the exit (measured by pacing distances)?
  - What is the lade made from?
  - How wide is it?
  - At what speed does water flow down the lade?
  - How is the flow of water controlled from the mill pond?
- How does the sluice work?
- What height is the pond in relation to the mill?
- How is the water returned to the river?
- Why is there a trap door in the lade?
- If the mill pond overfills, where does the overflow water go?

## What powers the mill machinery?

This involves careful study of the mill wheel which should be sketched, with notes added in order to establish

- What are the different parts of the wheel made of?
- Which parts of the wheel do you think will need replacing most frequently?
- At what point does the water hit the wheel?
- How does the water make the wheel turn?
- From where and how does the miller control starting and stopping the wheel?

## How does the machinery work?

Pupils could attempt this in a number of ways depending on their age and ability.

• Focus on how a particular part of the machinery works, i.e. the use of gears both to alter the speed at which the machinery turns and to shift from horizontal to vertical drive or the way the sack hoist can be switched on and off
• Study a particular piece of machinery that the drive reaches, especially the material, shape and design of the bedstone and runner stone as well as the dressing machinery and the shaking sieve
• Follow through the sequence of production by establishing key points through the following task which is attempted after pupils have seen a demonstration or the video.

# The Miller's Tale

Visitors often come to the mill.  What should the miller explain to them?

**1** 'Now this is what it's all about.
Let me tell you all about how these work.'

_____

_____

_____

**2** 'But there's lots to do before we can grind the oatmeal.
First we must dry it.  This is how we do it.'

_____

_____

_____

**3** 'Then we have to separate the husks from the grain kernel.
This is how we do it.'

_____

_____

**4** 'Now we must blow away the husks so that they don't
get mixed up with the grain.
The machine that does this works like this.'

_____

_____

**5** 'Now we're ready to feed the grain to the mill stones.
This is how it gets there.'

_____

_____

### What special features does this building have because it is a mill?

This work can be done by photographing, sketching or completing outlines showing the shape of the mill but leaving out all the details that have to be added in the course of the investigation. It is best to study the building once pupils have been shown how the machinery works and what is involved in grinding corn.

Some topics which might be discussed on site or on return to the classroom are
• why a weather vane is needed
• how hot damp air escapes from the kiln
• the positioning of doors and windows in relation to the work inside, e.g. the point at which sacks are lowered out of the mill
• the miller's house beside the mill
• signs of erosion

### How do past and present compare?

Pupils should be encouraged to listen to and find words to describe the sights and sounds of the mill site as it is today. What would they not have seen or heard 150 or 200 years ago? What might they have heard and seen in the past (in an age of horse-drawn traffic) that they do not hear today? How 'environmentally friendly' was the mill?

### What wildlife is attracted to the mill and its surrounding area?

Under supervision pupils could explore the area around the mill and the mill pond as a habitat for plants, animals, birds and fish. They could consider what effects there might be on the surrounding area if the mill stopped working.

### Following up fieldwork

UNDERSTANDING PEOPLE IN THE PAST

The mill provides
• evidence of the past to be observed, recorded and discussed.
• A sense of time and sequence in that a past way of life has been preserved going back to life in the nearby abbey. A mill time-line might be produced.
• opportunities to consider causes and consequences, change and continuity. For example, we still use oatmeal, but

are far less dependent on it given our access to other foods. Or we could examine the fact that the building of the mill has had consequences for the area.
• a context for considering aspects of heritage and conservation.

Historical understanding can be deepened by further research using early OS maps, census schedules, directories, Statistical Accounts, interviewing elderly people and searching for old photographs. Pupils could use the census to 'restore' the past population to its location ( on a copy of a first edition 25" Ordnance Survey map); or a word processed booklet on the mill could be produced.

PHOTO OF INSIDE OF MILL

UNDERSTANDING PEOPLE AND PLACE
The work on site involves thinking about the inter-action of people and place as well as using maps and places. A large colour-coded map of the area could be built up from the data gathered on fieldwork. An early Ordnance Survey map will allow an equivalent scene from over 100 years ago to be recorded.

SCIENCE AND TECHNOLOGY
The technology of waterpower could be studied further. Different designs of wheel could be investigated, and experiments set up to compare their respective merits. The drive and gears lend themselves to further study and practical experiments to fully grasp how they operate. How easy is it to grind oatmeal compared to other grains? It may be possible to plant and monitor the growth of different types of cereal crop.

EXPRESSIVE ARTS
The landowner could interview a

prospective miller to see how well he knows his trade. Pupils could design posters to draw visitors to the mill. Christmas cards, calendars, advertisements as they might once have appeared - all offer opportunities for art work.

ENGLISH LANGUAGE
All the relevant skills will be involved in discussing the visit, investigating and recording on site and from books, turning fieldwork notes into a systematic record and writing imaginative accounts of a person visiting or working at the mill in the past.

# Beyond Historic Scotland

In this book we have looked at a number of different ways historic sites can be exploited by teachers for implementing the 5-14 Environmental Studies guidelines. The application of these ideas is not exclusive to Historic Scotland sites and teachers are encouraged to think about visiting sites in the care of the National Trust for Scotland or independent trusts as well as historic houses in private ownership.

## The National Trust for

The National Trust for Scotland is the guardian of many of the finest treasures in the land ; whether they be mountains and lochs, castles and pictures or museums and family homes. The Trust has the close co-operation of local education authorities, and with the help of local education advisers has linked its education programme to the needs of the curriculum.

LEARNING ABOUT PRINTING TECHNIQUES AT ROBERT SMAIL'S PRINTING WORKS, INNERLEITHEN.

For further information contact the **Education Officer,** The National Trust for Scotland, 5 Charlotte Square, Edinburgh EH2 4DU. 0131- 226 5922

CHILDREN IN COSTUME AT CASTLE FRASER, GRAMPIAN.

1820'S MILLWORKERS' HOUSE, NEW LANARK MILLS.

**New Lanark Conservation Trust** offers a full range of educational services including guided visits, information and resource packs. Contact the Education Officer, New Lanark Conservation Trust, New Lanark Mills, Lanark ML11 9DB. 01555-661345

### The Buccleuch Heritage Trust

Bowhill House and Country Park, winner of the Sandford Award for Education in 1993, offers educational projects and courses based on the Buccleuch collections and all other aspects of the house as well as land-based educational projects. For further information contact Mrs Mary Carter, The Buccleuch Heritage Trust, Bowhill, Selkirk, Scotland TD7 5ET. 01750 20732

### Pluscarden Abbey

Benedictine monks welcome school parties to Pluscarden Abbey. For further information write to Pluscarden Abbey, Elgin, Moray IV30 3UA. 01343 - 890 257

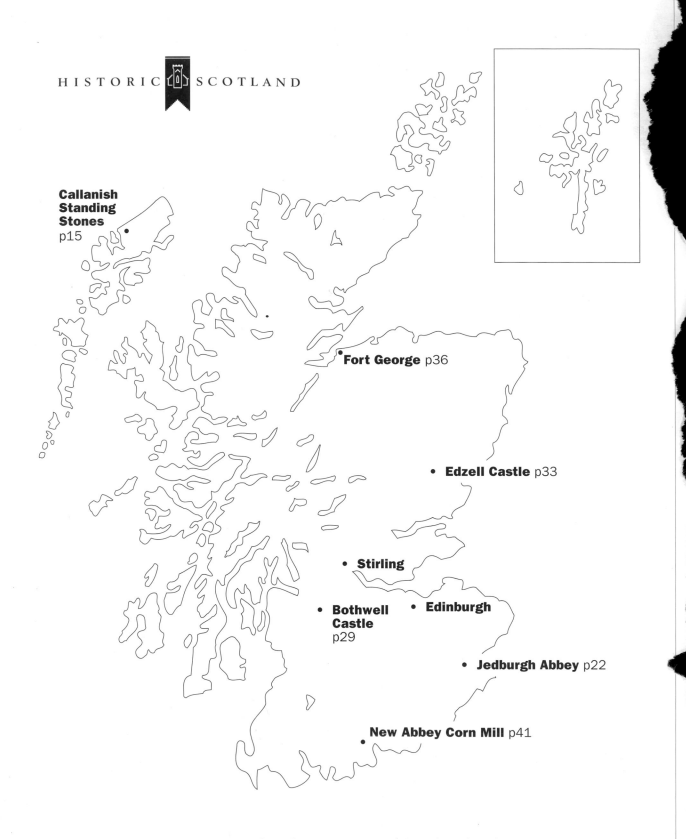

HISTORIC SCOTLAND

**Callanish
Standing
Stones**
p15

**Fort George** p36

**Edzell Castle** p33

**Stirling**

**Bothwell
Castle**
p29

**Edinburgh**

**Jedburgh Abbey** p22

**New Abbey Corn Mill** p41

*Historic Scotland sites covered in this book*